Rainbow Soup

adventures in poetry

Brian P. Cleary

illustrations by **Neal Layton**

M Millbrook Press / Minneapolis

Millbrook Press
A division of Lerner Publishing Group, Inc.
241 First Avenue North
Minneapolis, MN 55401 U.S.A.

Website address: www.lernerbooks.com

Library of Congress Cataloging-in-Publication Data

Cleary, Brian P., 1959—
    Rainbow soup : adventures in poetry / by Brian P. Cleary ; illustrations by Neal Layton.
        p.   cm.
    Includes index.
    Summary: An introduction to poetry that uses humorous poems, illustrations, and annotations to clarify terms and explain different types of poems, such as macaronic verse, concrete poems, and limericks.
    ISBN-13: 978—1—57505—597—8 (lib. bdg. : alk. paper)
    ISBN-10: 1—57505—597—X (lib. bdg. : alk. paper)
    1. Children's poetry, American. [1. American poetry.]
I. Layton, Neal, ill. II. Title.
PS3553.L39144R35 2004
808.1—dc21   2003004517

Manufactured in the United States of America
6 — PC — 7/1/12

To Owen,
who turned me on
to Shel Silverstein
—B. P. C.

For the sparrows
of Telephone Road
—N. L.

Welcome

Come romp with me amongst the words.
Come play amongst the phrases.
Swing and climb from pun to rhyme
And hop through versey mazes.
Swim through rivers thick with thought.
Rejoice from head to toe-etry.
Come beat your drums and shake your bums
And dance the dance of poetry.

Making the Best of a Bad Situation

Erik had a pair of heads,
And neither was becoming.
But happily he spent each day
Both whistling and humming.

*The **meter**, or rhythmic beat, of this type of poem is called **trochaic**. That's just a fancy word that tells us that the poem begins with the first syllable being "stressed," or emphasized, followed by the next syllable being "unstressed," or softer. See how you say "ER-ik" with more ooomph on the first part than the second? By the way, why can Erik both whistle and hum at the same time? Can you?*

SHHHHHH!

I've said too much already.
You know just what I mean.
If what's-his-name should find out,
There'd be an awful scene.

If he begins to ask around,
You haven't gotta clue.
We never had this talk, you hear,
If you see you-know-who!

Very Scary

Doors that creak while I'm in bed,
The vacant house beside us,
A story of a ghoul or ghost,
Our neighbor's pit bull, Midas,
The big, black crow upon the post
With eyes as dark as toffee—
None is half as frightening
As Mom before her coffee.

Rainbow Soup

Emma found an onion that was
Round and white and green.
Keisha brought the orangest carrot
Anyone had seen.

Luke had picked red peppers
And some juicy red tomatoes.
Lin Wu brought a big black pot
And four blue-skinned potatoes.

Patty poured in pasta
That was blue and gold and red.
Diego had a purple cabbage
(Bigger than his head!).

The yolks of two big eggs would add
Some yellow to the pot.
They diced and stirred and
Simmered it, till it was good and hot.

A little this and that
From every shape and color group—
It takes a bit of everything
To make a rainbow soup.

Making Money

My uncle ran a printing press—
A job he did with pride.
Along with cards and posters,
He made money on the side.

The government was so impressed
With all the work he'd done.
They've asked him to print license plates
Till twenty-twenty-one.

*The meter of this type of poem is called **iambic**. That tells us that it begins with the first syllable of the poem being "unstressed," or softer. Your ear does this naturally. You read "my UN-cle," right? You stress the second syllable instead of the first syllable. Do you get the joke about printing license plates?*

When I Am No Longer

They can give my arms to the army,
Take my eyes of blue,
And give my knees to the needy,
But my heart goes out to you.

They can take my shins to a shindig,
Hitch my thumb for a ride,
And give my wrists to a 'ristocrat,
But my heart stays at your side.

They'll give my nose to the nosy,
When they're taking me apart.
They'll give my hands to the handyman,
But you shall get my heart.

My ears will go to the eerie—
It's scary, but it's true.
The rest can go to science,
But my heart goes out to you.

Spanish Lessons
(Easy as 1,2,3)

U-NO, a spider's on my nose!
It's something I must face—
I'd like a DOS of courage
But I haven't got a TRES.

How to pronounce these Spanish words:
Uno: Sounds like "ooh-no."
Dos: Sounds like "dose."
Tres: Sounds like "trace."

Macaronic verses *are rhyming poems in which words from other*
languages are used. What English words do the highlighted Spanish
and French words sound like?

What Can I C'est?

My auntie Michelle is big in the BON
(As well as the hip and the thigh).
And when she exhales, OUI haul out our sails
And ride on the wind of VERSAILLES.

How to pronounce these French words:
C'est: Sounds like "say."
Bon: Sounds like "bone" (with a very soft "n").
Oui: Sounds like "we."
Versailles: Sounds like "ver-SIGH."

Rest in Pieces

Here lies Owen Matthew.
He was found about the plain.
He caught bugs and butterflies
And tried to catch a train.

Tall Tales

Here lies Francis Kotlin,
At 81 years old.
He claimed to be a fisherman
But couldn't catch a cold.

ATCHOO!

Debtor's Grave

Even though Joe's gone from here,
His debts are monumental—
The suit that he was buried in
Turned out to be a rental.

2 LN

LN, dear, sweet LN,
B4 U, now I stand.
2 me U R a QTpie.
Y don't U take my hand?

The NV of the others
U N I would always B.
I M D perfect 1 4 U—
Just U 8 N C!

English Lessons

If it's true "I sit" today
But yesterday "I sat,"
Could it be said "I bit" today,
But in the past, "I bat?"

And with that bat, if I should hit,
Shall it be said, "I've hitten?"
For if that bat should bite me,
You can bet your butt, I'm bitten.

And if that bite should mend itself,
One might proclaim, "I'm healed."
But people ask me how it felt
And never how it feeled.

For those of us who learned English as our primary language, we sure are lucky. It's one of the trickiest languages to learn. How many grammar mistakes do you notice in the poem above?

How People Came to America*

Some swum.

*At eight letters, believed to be the second shortest poem ever.

What I'd Do If a Burglar Broke into My House**

I'd hide.

*__**At six letters, believed to be the shortest poem ever.__*

Stop Awhile

Geraldine, the Grammar Queen,
Knows all about the comma—
She separates each phrase, as in,
Your dad,
Your sis,
Your mama,
By dropping in the curly mark
To make us briefly pause.
Yes, Geraldine loves commas,
In a sentence, phrase, or clause.

Commas here,
Commas there,
She just can't live without 'em.
She made a great big billboard
Just to tell the town about 'em.
She put a ten-foot comma
On the billboard,
And she reckoned
That she could make the
Traffic stop

,

If only for a second.

Why would the cars stop briefly for a moment when they saw the giant comma?

Ask Your Teacher

There is only one state
In this country so great
That can rhyme with the state of Nebraska.

I don't recall which,
But my teacher, Miss Fitch,
Will certainly know, so Alaska.

The Bad Diet

A young girl named Lottie
Was born with no body
And later, in dieting, shed
The rest of her weight,
And now it's too late—
Should have quit while
She was
Still
A
Head.

A Real Education

My dad went into business—
My college fund he spent.
He bought a perfume company
But hasn't made a scent.

Bananas

You're tasty and nutritious
In dessert or with a meal.
You come without a core or seeds
But always have a peel.

*A **pun** is a play on words, or a little joke using words or phrases that sound alike.*

Nonsense Rhyme
(Who's the Mindless One?)

One tall midget reached up high,
Touched the ground above the sky,
Tied his loafers, licked his tongue,
And told about the bee he stung.

He painted, then, an oval square,
The color of the bald man's hair,
And in the painting you could hear
What's undetected by the ear.

The lame boy ran to catch a train
That flew from Kansas south to Maine.
Upon the trip, before he went,
He wrote the letters he had sent.

Some day you may read this rhyme
And you may say I have no mind,
Although I wrote it, this is true,
I haven't read it—unlike you!

This poem is written in **couplets**, *meaning the first two lines rhyme with each other, the next two rhyme with each other, and so on.*

Relatively Speaking

Jane is my dad's
Second wife's second daughter,
And Josh is my mother's first son.
He came from my mother's
First marriage, to Terry
(Although it was his second one).

Billy's the offspring of Dad
And his first wife,
The one who would later elope
With one of Mom's exes—a doctor from Texas—
Who always smelled strongly of soap.

There surely are twists in the trunk and the branches
That make up our family tree.
And though it's bemusing,
Complex, and confusing,
Without it, we wouldn't have me.

*In line 4 of the middle **stanza** (stanza basically means a paragraph of poetry), I used a device called **internal rhyme** by rhyming "exes" and "Texas" on the same line.*

Syl-la-bles

A name such as Julia
Often will fulia.
Is it two beats or three?

Beats me.

Mr. and Mrs.

She Mrs. him while he's away
And thinks of how he's kissed her.
The few times he's been out of town,
He tells her that he's Mr.

Deliver Me

I like pizza when I wake,
Not eggs or toast or coffee cake.
I like pizza in my lunch.
After school, it's great to munch.

I like pizza at the mall,
In a restaurant, house, or hall.
I like pizza for dessert.
I've even licked it off my shirt.

I like pizza by the sheet,
Filled with sauce and cheese and meat.
I like pizza by the pie,
Crisp 'n' flat or thick 'n' high.

Sausage, peppers, double cheese,
Everything but anchovies,
Pepperoni, even chicken,
All these get my lips a-lickin'.

I like pizza hot or cold,
Nice and fresh or three days old.
And though I'd like to tell you more—
The pizza guy is at my door.

TREBOR! ROBERT!

Robert Trebor

Since Robert Trebor learned to spell,
He's always loved his name.
'Cause if you write it left or right,
It comes out just the same.

He yells it to the canyons,
And he sings it to the blackbirds.
"My name is so amazing.
You can say it front or backwards."

Words or phrases that are spelled the same way backward and forward are called **palindromes**. *A palindrome can be a phrase like "A Toyota," a word like "kayak," a name like "Hannah," or even a number like "747." Try writing one of these with a friend, and you'll be putting the "pal" into palindrome!*

Brother, Can You Spare a Rhyme?

Brother, can you spare a rhyme?
I'm down upon my luck.
Seems Nature gave me room and board
And not one single buck.

But if you read some verse to me
Or tell a tale or two,
Then I'll continue wealthily
With what I've learned from you.

When folks give up their money,
They have less—you get the pit-chur.
But share with me a rhyme,
And leave us both a little richer.

The Ballad of Brady O'Grady
(or It Could Happen to You!)

Brady O'Grady didn't like schools,
Didn't like teachers,
Didn't need rules,
Wouldn't take orders,
Couldn't sit still.
Brady O'Grady had his fill.

Brady O'Grady decided he'd quit.
He said, "I don't need it—
Not one little bit!"
Yanked out his bike
From the bicycle rack.
Brady O'Grady never looked back.

Brady O'Grady watched TV
Nineteen hours
And slept just three.
Spent two more
Playing video games—
Brady O'Grady fried his brains.

Brady O'Grady, 20 years later,
Teeth like corn
And skin like a tater.
Ears so dirty,
He might have to weed 'em—
Brady O'Grady got his freedom.

THE
END

to e. e. cummings

thank you for your lively verse
and playful, quirky prose.
you wrote of nature, war,
and love, the

r
a
i
n
d
r
o
p
s

and the rose.

a modern-thinking artist,
with an intellect immense,
if you're not in every classroom,
it's a capital offense.

thank you for undreary theory,
style, wit, and grace.
your books are always on my shelf
(tucked in my lower case).

e.e. cummings (he had his name legally changed to have no capital letters!) was a poet and modern artist who used punctuation and type in interesting ways. He would often put "non" or "un" in front of a word, as I did in the final stanza. Do you get the double meaning of "lower case" in the last line?

Crazy

They send me to bed
When I'm not even tired
And wake me when I'm fast asleep.
They send me to school
And make me eat veggies
And ask me to vacuum and sweep.

I'm forced to take showers,
Although I'm still clean
From the one that I took just last week.
They also have told me
I can't keep the snake that I found
Yesterday in the creek.

They've said that my bedroom
Resembles a train wreck
And even suggested I'm lazy.
But get this—
I know that it's hard to believe—
I really do love 'em like crazy.

Masculine rhyme *occurs when the rhyming word either has one syllable, like "week" and "creek," or when the rhyme falls on the last syllable of a two-syllable word or phrase, as in "asleep" and "and sweep." The stress or accent needs to be on the final (or only) syllable.*

33

Tuna Fish
(Spread the Word)

Tuna fish, tuna fish!
Can't wait till lunch
At noon-a-fish!
October, March,
And June-a-fish!
I love your tender ways.

Tuna fish, tuna fish!
There's just no way
To ruin-a-fish!
A work of art—that's tuna fish—
A Monet on mayonnaise!

Tuna fish, tuna-fish!
On knife and fork
And spoon-a-fish,
You take me to
The moon-a-fish!
I'll love you all my days.

Falling for Amber

I think that Amber's pretty,
So in school I tried to find her.
I saw her on the stairs, and then
I sneaked up close behind her.
I reached up on my tiptoes,
And I tried to steal a kiss,
But I don't think she liked it
'Cause
I
Ended
Up

Like this.

I'll Love You Till the Butterflies

I'll love you till
The butterflies,
Until the sugar bowls.
I'll love you till
The kitchen sinks,
And celery stalks the rolls.

I'm yours until
The bacon strips,
Until the fireflies.
I'm yours until
The ocean seas,
Just like it had two eyes.

The day you see a pocket watch
A barn dance all night long,
The day a grape jams
On the stage,
You know that I'll be gone.

Irish Peace Talks

There once was a schoolgirl from Galway,
Who said to her lad on a fall day,
"If I find you starin'
At Maggie or Erin,
They'll be scrapin' you offa the hallway."

These little five-line verses are called **limericks**. *They're usually funny and have a specific rhyme pattern. Lines 1, 2, and 5 rhyme with each other, while lines 3 and 4 rhyme together in a different sound. The longer lines of the poem tend to be 8 to 10 syllables. Can you write one?*

The C@ Was Out of H&

A sleepwalking calico c@
Some days walks away from her m@.
She strolls all about
The city without
Having even a clue where she's @.

One evening, completely unpl&,
She walked to a tavern to st&
At the bar on this outing,
And was heard to be shouting,
"I can lick any c@ in the l&."

Having trouble figuring this one out? Just sound out the letters before the signs for "at" and "and." See how it reads? How many other words could you come up with like these? Also, can "lick" have two meanings? This poem is basically a double limerick in terms of form.

Oh, to Be Nine Again

Oh, to be nine again!
I would recline again,
Under a pine again—
Sleep now and then.

I'd romp like a child should—
Hike in the wild wood.
I sure miss my childhood,
Now that I'm ten.

Harry Had a Little Scam

Harry had a little scam.
He'd fleece you for your dough.
Everywhere that Harry went
The cops were sure to show.

This is something called a **parody** of a famous poem. A
parody is like a funny version of something that was
originally serious. What poem does this one sound like?
If "fleece" in this case means swindle, or steal, could
"fleece" also have another meaning? If so, what does it
have to do with the original poem?

My Cat Bytes

Some cats like to prowl,
And some even growl,
While others would rather take naps.
But my Mrs. Mittens—
An Internet kitten—is
Fonder of laptops than laps.

Unlike other cats,
This one downloads and chats
And is constantly checking her e-mail.
An ad she has posted
Has recently boasted
She's a young single, Siamese female.

With paws soft and quick,
She'll type and she'll click,
Do some research or maybe some shopping.
She bookmarks new sites.
She surfs and she writes,
Or she'll scan in some photos for swapping.

It's simply absurd.
She's an Internet nerd,
Who ignores all the rest of the house.
What cat would admit
It would ever see fit
To enjoy so much time with a mouse?

MEOW!

Fall

Early in autumn,
Early at night,
I'm early in bed
'Neath the dim moonlight.

I called God and caught 'im
At home for the night.
"Thank you," I said,
"For this cool dark night."

Spring

Late in the season,
Late in the day,
The sun's sinking low
On the Western bay.

I whispered to God,
"Can you show me a way
To bottle the glow
Of this warm, spring day?"

Horizon

Outintheeastwherethesunisarisin',there's

In a **concrete poem**, the poem itself takes on the shape of its subject (such as a picket fence or giraffe). The letters, words, or symbols are arranged on the page into a picture. Notice how, if you simply read these poems out loud to someone, they'd miss part of the experience?

alinejustlikethis,andit'scalledahorizon.

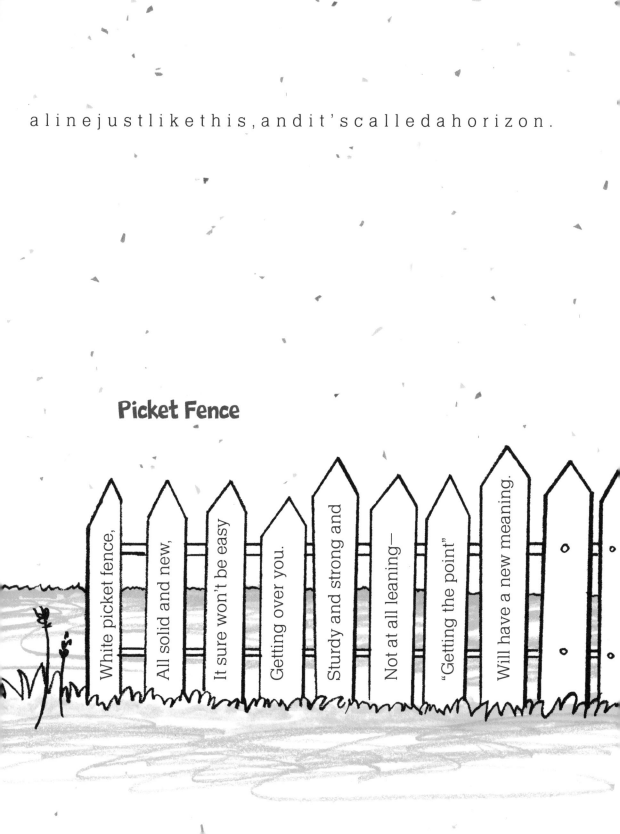

Picket Fence

White picket fence,
All solid and new,
It sure won't be easy
Getting over you.
Sturdy and strong and
Not at all leaning—
"Getting the point"
Will have a new meaning.

"I wonder," said Mark, "if the big brown dog has a bite that lives up to his bark." If you'd like to know, you can question the dog, but there's no way to question Mark.

No Question, Mark

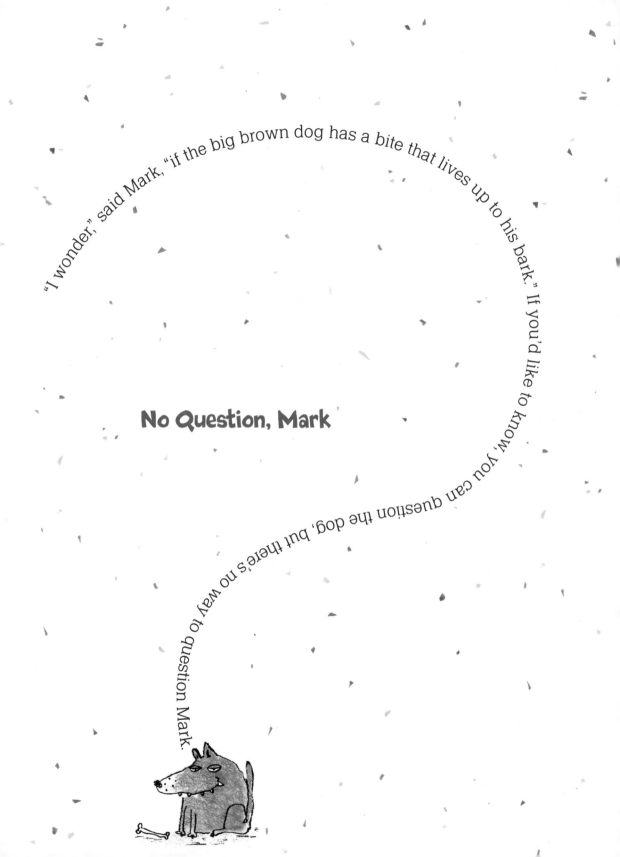

Illiteracy Hurts

One day a bear trap snared her leg, squeezing it tight like parentheses.

Caution! No Trespassing! Please Keep Out! Patricia could not make sense of these.

The Giraffe

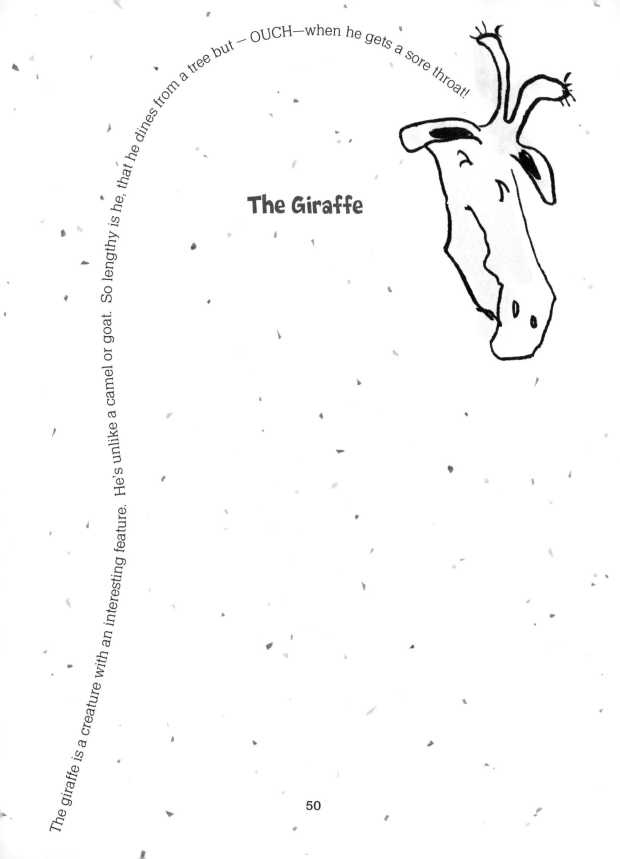

The giraffe is a creature with an interesting feature. He's unlike a camel or goat. So lengthy is he, that he dines from a tree but – OUCH—when he gets a sore throat!

Tennis Ball

Tennis ball
Off the wall.

51

Sneezin's Greetings

Haiku . . . Gesundheit!
It seems like every summer
My nostrils explode.

Report Card

Four days of the year,
One tiny piece of paper
Turns my stomach sour.

Haiku *is a Japanese form of three-line poetry in which the top and bottom lines typically have 5 syllables and the middle line has 7. Quite often the subject of haiku deals with nature or the seasons.*

Seasons

Of all the seasons,
The one that I like the best
Is surely baseball.

January

Dad will remind us
That we shouldn't try to heat
The whole neighborhood.

The Guitar

The guitar is just as comfortable
In blue jeans or in tails.
He's equally at home with jazzy riffs
Or bluesy wails.

His home can be the coffeehouse,
The front porch, or the bar,
The opera or the classroom
Or the hood of Daddy's car.

Amplified, he rocks the house.
Unplugged, he can be dreamy,
As soothing as a lullaby,
Or sultry, hot, and steamy.

Whether he's strummed or picked or plucked,
That won't make him start fretting.
He's just as excited if he gets invited
To a festival, concert, or wedding.

Personification *is what we call giving human qualities to something, like a guitar, that isn't living (an inanimate object). How has this poem treated the guitar like a person? "Fretting," which is seen in the third to last line in this poem, has a double meaning. It can relate to the fingering on the neck of the guitar, or it can mean to be worried or anxious.*

The Trumpet

The trumpet is loud,
Triumphant, and proud.
It's bold and incredibly brassy.
It can sound cool and shady,
Behave like a lady,
Or be guttural, gutsy, or classy.

The trumpet was born
To blow its own horn.
It's been played both
By princes and peasants.
The coronet's cousin,
With your lips a-buzzin',
Is ideal for announcing
Your presence.

Notice the rhymed words "classy" and "brassy," as well as "peasants" and "presence." This type of rhyme is called **feminine rhyme**. *It's a rhyme of two or more syllables in which the first syllable is the strongest. So when you rhyme "boil it" with "toilet," you can mention that you were in the feminine rhyme phase of your poetry writing career.*

The Cello

If the cello
Were a fellow,
He'd be rich and
Deep and mellow—
Shoulders wide as Monticello—
Humming warmly as he strolls.

Brown or tan
But never yellow,
More like casserole
Than Jell-O,
Maybe Mushrooms Portabello,
With a side of buttered rolls.

Warm in tone,
He doesn't bellow.
He may kiss
But never tell—oh,
Gently whispering, the cello,
Is a comfort to our souls.

*Any idea what Monticello is? Take out a
nickel, and look on the back of it. What
famous American lived there? Hint: Look at
the front of the same nickel!*

Going in Reverse

Backwards Bob would say good-bye
When folks were walking in.
He'd put his shoes on, then his pants,
And then he'd take a swim.

He'd sleep all day and work all night
And drive home in reverse.
When they saw Bob, pedestrians
And cars would all disperse.

They all thought he'd outgrow his ways,
But what they couldn't know,
Is that he gets younger every year,
'Cause he died long ago.

You Try and Rhyme Something With Purple

Penny pulled and Patrick pushed
A giant ball of yarn.
It was 20 feet across and white and purple.
They argued all the day
About whose efforts moved the ball.
Couldn't tell you if it was his push or her pull.

Purple is one of the most difficult words to rhyme in the English language. Once in a while if you use two words, you can create a sound that gets close. Do you have any suggestions?

Ode to Peanut Butter and Jelly

PB&J,
You're more than OK—
You're the star of America's lunches.
It's clear with each bite
That your texture's just right—
You're perfect between sips and crunches.

PB&J,
In the whole U.S.A.,
No other concoction can beat you.
You're loved by the millions
Of Jackies and Jillians
Who can't wait till lunchtime to eat you.

Mixed Marriage

A centipede married a chicken one day.
They sure made an interesting pair.
And when they had kids,
They had enough drumsticks
To feed any crowd, anywhere!

Raindrops

Rain,
Like tears,
Is running
Down my window:
Pain.

Cloudy Skies

My
Shadow
Has never
Gotten to meet
You.

*A **lantern** is a five-line, unrhymed form of poetry, which is shaped like a Japanese lantern. Like haiku, it often deals with nature. The first line has 1 syllable, the second 2, then 3, 4, and finally 1.*

I've Had a Really Lousy Day

My mom wrote a note
That my dog ate my homework,
And then my dog ate my mom's note.
I opened his mouth and got out a flashlight,
So I could look down in his throat.

With the batteries shot,
I gave up all hope, and
Decided to dress for the day.
My pants were too short, my shirt had a juice stain
That looked like a map of Green Bay.

Too late for breakfast,
I scarfed down an apple,
That had in it half of a worm,
Which might explain why it was so hard to chew—
The food seemed to constantly squirm.

The rain soaked me through,
And a car almost hit me.
It's amazing that I'm still alive.
I've had an incredibly terrible day—

And it's only 8:45!

Without Contrast

Short and tall,
Big and small,
There is no spring without the fall.
Good and bad,
Happy, sad,
You need a mom to make a dad.
Up and down,
A smile, a frown,
Silence is without a sound.
Rude, polite,
Day or night,
Without the dark, there is no light.

Stop and go,
A friend, a foe,
Nothing's high till something's low.
Right or wrong,
Weak or strong,
Till something's short, there's nothing long.
Early, late,
Love and hate,
Without the curved, there is no straight.
Slow and fast,
Future, past—
There's nothing here without contrast.

The Cigarette

Smokin'.
Chokin'.
Coughin'.
Coffin.

Nose Flood

"I chuckled so hard, milk came out of my nose,"
Said my math teacher, Mrs. Mantunkenny.
"What's hard to explain," she said with some pain,
"Is that I had not even drunk any."

Triple rhyme is simply a three-syllable rhyme, as in this poem, which rhymes the last 3 syllables of the teacher's name, "Mantunkenny," with the phrase "drunk any" (which is also 3 syllables).

Lettuce Pray (A Ballad to Salad)

There's been many a song
About love that's gone wrong.
There are poems of love found and lost.
There is verse by the score
About friendship and war
By Shakespeare and Gershwin and Frost.

One topic's been slighted,
And it shall be righted—
There should be a ballad to salad.
Just because you are doomed
To be tossed and consumed,
Does that make you any less valid?

At a picnic or a dance
In the country of France,
You are eaten after dinner, not before.
Whether iceberg or romaine,
Folks from Mexico and Spain
Tell their waiters, "We'd like salad, por favor."

In a restaurant or pavilion,
You have served us by the billion.
You go great with both a hot dog or soufflé.
In shorts or with a suit on,
Every cucumber and crouton
I have eaten from you brightened up my day.

Winter

Wind whipping white little swirls of snow.
Icicles are reaching to the drifts that grow below.
Night is falling early, and dawn is sleeping in.
Time for cocoa from a cup and cookies from a tin,
Extra-toasty blankets on an extra-cozy bed,
Rosy cheeks and frosty peaks and riding on a sled.

This poetic form is called an **acrostic**. *In this type of poem, the first or last letters of each line, when read vertically, will form a word or phrase. It's not necessary for an acrostic poem to rhyme. You can try it either way!*

We're Going to the Villa, Nell

School is over, sounds the bell,
And that means summer has begun.
We're going to the villa, Nell.

Where we'll catch toads and mackerel
And swim all day beneath the sun.
School is over, sounds the bell.

The voice of our Aunt Isabel
Will blend with Dad's accordion.
We're going to the villa, Nell.

Where watermelon twilights fell
Since we were two and one.
School is over, sounds the bell.

I'll race you to the old stone well,
And Mom can say which one has won.
We're going to the villa, Nell.

"It's snowing fireflies," you'll yell,
As crickets croon and rapids run.
School is over, sounds the bell.
We're going to the villa, Nell.

*This is a French form of poetry, called a **villanelle** (note the pun). The villanelle is always nineteen lines long. Line 1 is repeated on lines 6, 12, and 18. Line 3 is repeated on lines 9, 15, and 19. The second line of each stanza rhymes all the way down the poem. Use my poem as a blueprint, repeating in exactly the same places and rhyming the middle line. The cool part is, that once you've written those two lines, you'll be about halfway done!*

My Calendar

I found we had a test today.
But I had written "rest today,"
Upon this page just yest-a-day,
And so I'm not prepared.

If I had written "test today,"
I could've done my best today!
If only it were yest-a-day,
I wouldn't be so scared.

Five

Danny has three extra legs
(One right and two above).
He has some trouble walking,
But his pants fit like a glove.

Making Ripples

🐐 - T out and look up 2 the morning SK + 👁

🐝 + 4 u ☆ + T each day, &

ask yourself what U 🛢 do @ school, @ 🏠 ,

@ play, 2 make this day a better 1 4 some

1 N + 👂 or far. & the 🌐 📜 🐝

a better PL + ♠ because of who U R.

This type of picture poem is called a **rebus**. A rebus could take the form of a poem (as it is here), a paragraph, sentence, or even a riddle! In this type of poem, words or syllables are replaced by pictures or symbols. Can you "translate" this one?

Jump Rope Song

Popcorn,
Pizza,
Watermelon pie,
Bug juice,
Baseball,
Skeeter on your thigh.

Kickball,
Kickstand,
Sleepin' on the roof.
Molly has a collie,
And he goes, "Woof, woof!"

Brother's on the back porch.
Sister's on the swing.
Mother's in the maple tree awaitin' for spring.
Baby's in the buggy.
Daddy's in the den.
But we all get together when we count to ten . . .

6th Grade Grill

Benny buttered bagels.
Charlie chopped the cheese.
Samantha made the stir-fry
And some other things Chinese.

Ashley made the applesauce.
Dylan did the dishes.
Maddy made the muffins,
And they turned out just delicious.

Wendy washed the windows.
Bobby bussed the booths.
They sure worked well together
For a group of untrained youths.

Kaitlyn cleaned the kitchen.
Sarah swept the floor.
They sauteed, simmered, stirred, and served,
And then they worked some more.

Despite their work, they had to close,
Declaring bankruptcy,
'Cause no one ran the register,
And everyone ate free.

Alliteration *is the occurrence of the same sound (often the same letter) in words, which are near each other. In every stanza here, there are examples of alliteration, from "Benny buttered bagels" in the first stanza to "ran the register" in the final one. "Kaitlyn cleaned" also counts as alliteration because although the words begin with different letters, both have the same sound.*

Mr. Couldashouldawoulda

Mr. Couldashouldawoulda
Never took the time
To learn the sax
Or pet the yaks
Or try his hand at rhyme.

Mr. Couldashouldawoulda
Couldn't fit it in
When friends would say,
"Come on let's play
Or dance or paint or swim."

Mr. Couldashouldawoulda
Never got around
To catching frogs
Or rolling logs
Or sleeping on the ground.

Mr. Couldashouldawoulda
Just turned 64.
He wishes that he
Couldashouldawoulda
Done some more.

The I-Know-What's-Ailin'-Me Blues

I ain't got no measles on me.
I ain't got no measles on me.
I ain't got no measles as you can plainly see.
I ain't got no measles on me.

I ain't got no strep throat in me.
I ain't got no strep throat in me.
I ain't got no strep throat, said ol' Doc MacAvee.
I ain't got no strep throat in me.

Ain't got no bronchitis in me.
Ain't got no bronchitis in me.
Ain't got no bronchitis, arthritis, or bursitis.
Ain't got no things -itis in me.

Doc says ain't nothin' wrong with me.
Doc says ain't nothin' wrong with me.
In his vestibule today,
He sent me back to school today.
Doc says ain't nothin' wrong with me.

*The **blues** is an African-American musical art form. The first and second lines in each verse are almost always identical, and the subject of the song usually has to do with something that makes the singer sad or "blue."*

Sporting Kids

Soccer kids are such a kick—
They always have a ball.
Hockey kids are oh-so cool,
Especially when they fall.
Baseball kids will sacrifice
To help their teammate score.
And kids whose game is basketball?
They dribble on the floor!
Football kids are in a rush
To end up on the ground.
And the alleys and the gutters
Are where bowling kids are found.
A stroke is good for swimming kids
And golfing kids as well.
But kids who run cross-country?
Why, they just run like . . .
Heck.

My Brother Joe

My brother Joe steals.
My brother Joe hits.
I know he's not safe when he's out.
There's sometimes foul play
In the things that he does.
Can you tell what I'm talking about?

This poem is also a riddle.
For you to solve it, you need
to know two meanings for
some of these words.

I Babysat (Once)

I was pushing the buggy one day,
When my grip on the handle gave way,
And it started to roll
Downhill out of control,
With my sister still snoozing away.

She rolled through the center of town,
Still asleep through the deafening sound,
Of barks and bow-wow-as
Of the beagles, Chihuahuas,
And mutts at the city dog pound.

Past Main Street and Elm rolled my sister.
It's amazing that all the cars missed her.
She moved with the ease
Of a cool evening breeze
But the speed of a level 3 twister.

I found her off Highway 19,
Having gone through a car wash machine.
With a lemony smell
(They had waxed her as well),
I brought her back home nice and clean.

Joy

Joy looks like fireworks against a night sky.
Joy tastes like the first crunch into an ear of corn.
Joy sounds like the circus coming to town.
Joy smells like popcorn.
Joy feels like running home on the last day of school.

*A **sensory poem** uses your five senses. It takes an abstract subject (something you can't see or feel, such as love, fear, or anger) and tells the reader what it tastes like, looks like, smells like, feels like, and sounds like.*

Translation

When Alex says he "shook a tower,"
What he means is "took a shower."

He'll point and say "a flutter by,"
And then we'll see a butterfly.

He once proclaimed, "Hey, belly jeans"
When he found a stash of jelly beans.

But when he says he pepped in stew,
We'll tell him he should wipe his shoe.

A **spoonerism** mixes up the first sound of two or more words in a phrase. It gets its name from the Reverend William A. Spooner, a minister and educator who was famous for this type of verbal slipup.

My Three Dogs

My dog Moxie runs like the rain,
Growls like a lion,
And soars like a plane.

My dog Izzy is as bright as the sun,
As quiet as a lamb,
And as true as a nun.

My dog Connor is as big as a mountain,
As slow as erosion,
And squirts like a fountain.

*A **simile** compares two unlike things (such as a smile and sunshine) using the words "like" or "as." "Her smile is like sunshine" is an example of a simile. Can you find the similes in this poem?*

Love and Peace

Tyler likes Hannah.
Hannah likes Lance.
Lance likes the girl
With the leopard-print pants.
She likes Isaiah.
Isaiah likes Tess.
She likes Antonio,
Justin, and Jess.
Zack likes Melissa,
Who just likes to dance.
Shelley likes David,
And David likes Nance.
There's love in the air
Of room 229,
But peace is a little bit
Harder to find.

Babysitter's Song

8:00 P.M.

Good-night, little Rory,
And teddy bear, Cory.
I'll read you a story,
Then "lights out," OK?

8:37 P.M.

It's beddy-bye dream time,
Your lullaby theme time,
Not "let's-cry-and-scream" time.
So what do you say?

9:22 P.M.

I want to call Gracie,
And Stephen, and Tracey,
So upstairs you'll stay, see?
Stop bothering me!

10:04 P.M.

C'mon kid, quit cryin'.
You're not even tryin'.
I'm beat, and I'm dyin'
To watch some TV.

10:54 P.M.

Look, I know you're cranky,
So go grab your blankie.
I wave the white hankie—
Come stay here with me.

Thank You, Dear Reader
(And Now a Word from Our Poems)

Thank you, Dear Reader, for playing with us.
You really were wonderful company.
You climbed and explored since you skittered aboard.
We sure hope that you didn't bump-a-knee!
Poems, like people, enjoy getting out—
We like to be seen now and then.
When books are shut tight, we don't get much light,
So take us out now and again.
Show us to family and share us with friends—
Just don't leave us up on your shelf.
And poetry's not just a spectator sport,
So why don't you try some yourself?

86

Index of Titles

Index of Definitions